Conspiracy Theories? Or Spoiler Alerts!

2023 In Review...

By L. Robinson

1 Introduction: Unveiling the Shadows - Setting the stage for a journey into the world of modern conspiracy theories.

2 The UAP Enigma: Delving into the ongoing mystery and government responses to Unidentified Aerial Phenomena.

3 The Deepfake Dilemma: Exploring the implications of deepfake technology in media and politics.

4 Surveillance Society: Investigating the expansion of global surveillance networks by governments and corporations.

5 Vaccine Controversies: Examining the microchipping conspiracy theories surrounding COVID-19 vaccines.

6 Cyber Shadows: Analyzing the hidden world of state-sponsored cyberattacks and their global impact.

7 The AI Influence: Unraveling the theories about AI algorithms manipulating public opinion and election outcomes.

8 Secrets: Investigating claims of clandestine climate manipulation projects.

9 Space Race Mysteries: Probing into the

alleged secrets and misinformation in contemporary space exploration efforts.

10 Pandemic's Hidden Origin: Delving into the contentious debates about the true origins of COVID-19.

11 5G Fears: Unpacking the health and surveillance conspiracy theories linked to 5G technology.

12 Cryptocurrency Conspiracies: Analyzing theories around governmental regulation and control of digital currencies.

13 Facial Recognition Fears: Exploring the implications of AI in mass surveillance.

14 Suppressed Energy Technologies: Investigating claims of hidden advancements in energy suppressed by traditional industries.

15 Mind Control Technologies: Examining theories about the development of technology capable of reading and influencing minds.

16 Alien Encounters Concealed: Investigating claims about government cover-ups of extraterrestrial contacts.

17 Health Data Dilemmas: Analyzing privacy concerns in the era of digital health records.

18 Biological Experimentation Allegations: Uncovering theories about covert government biological experiments.

19 Social Media's Hidden Hand: Exploring claims of manipulation and disinformation spread through social platforms.

Are You Ready?

In an era where the line between reality and fiction blurs, where truths are often stranger than fiction, and where the shadows of doubt loom large over the most ordinary of events, "Conspiracy Theories or Spoiler Alerts! 2023 in Review" emerges as a beacon in the darkness. This book is not just a collection of stories; it is a journey into the heart of the unknown, the misunderstood, and the deliberately obscured.

As you turn these pages, you embark on an expedition through the intricate labyrinths of modern conspiracy theories. Each chapter is a doorway into a different realm, where the possibilities are as limitless as they are unsettling. From the mysterious depths of 5G technology and its alleged links to global health crises to the enigmatic world of cryptocurrency and the power struggles hidden within its code, every narrative is a thread in the vast tapestry of contemporary myths and realities.

But this book is more than a mere exposé of the year's most talked-about conspiracies. It is an invitation to question, to delve deeper, and to look beyond the surface. It challenges you to sift through layers of misinformation and half-truths to uncover the spoiler alerts - the hidden truths that lie within these widely debated theories.

Authored by L. Robinson, a name synonymous with unraveling the complex webs of modern mythology, this book is a testament to the human desire to find answers in a world that often offers none. Robinson's writing is not just informative; it is a gripping narrative that captures the essence of each conspiracy, offering insights that are as enlightening as they are provocative.

As the world continues to reel from the aftermath of a global pandemic, the rise of advanced technologies, and the ever-shifting sands of geopolitics, "Conspiracy Theories or Spoiler Alerts! 2023 in Review" is both timely and timeless. It is a reflection of our times and a mirror held up to our collective psyche, revealing our deepest fears and our unquenchable thirst for understanding.

Prepare to be drawn into a world where every corner hides a story, every story a puzzle, and every puzzle a piece of the grand mosaic of our contemporary existence. Welcome to "Conspiracy Theories or Spoiler Alerts! 2023 in Review" – your guide to the mysteries that have captivated and confounded us in these unprecedented times.

Is This The Beginning for You?

Discover the intriguing world of "Conspiracy Theories or Spoiler Alerts," a compelling book series by L. Robinson that delves deep into the mysteries and truths behind some of the most talked-about conspiracy theories. These books are not just a collection of speculative tales; they are a journey through the intricate maze of historical and contemporary theories, exploring the fine line between fiction and reality.

In this series, L. Robinson masterfully uncovers the hidden truths behind various conspiracy theories, providing readers with a thought-provoking analysis that challenges conventional thinking. From exploring government cover-ups and secret societies to unraveling the mysteries of technological advancements and global events, these books are a must-read for anyone fascinated by the unknown and the unexplained.

Whether you are a skeptic or a believer, the "Conspiracy Theories or Spoiler Alerts" series offers a unique perspective on the world's most intriguing conspiracy theories. Each book is meticulously researched, presenting a balanced view that combines historical facts with compelling narrative, ensuring that every reader is left questioning what they thought they knew.

Don't miss out on this captivating series. Purchase your copies of the "Conspiracy Theories or Spoiler Alerts" books today and embark on an eye-opening journey that blurs the line between myth and reality.

Conspiracy Theories or Spoiler Alerts?: 20 Tales of Deception!

Conspiracy Theories or Spoiler Alerts: The UAP Files

Available Now At Amazon.com and All Major Book Retailers

CHAPTER 1: INTRODUCTION: UNVEILING THE SHADOWS

As the world whirls into another year, it brings with it a tapestry of tales, some woven with threads of truth, others shrouded in the mists of mystery. In "Conspiracy Theories or Spoiler Alerts! 2023 in Review," we embark on a journey to unravel these narratives, exploring the intricate and often hidden world of modern conspiracy theories.

A World Enthralled by Conspiracies

The human fascination with conspiracy theories is not a new phenomenon, yet it has found renewed vigor in the digital age. This chapter sets the stage for our exploration, delving into the psychology behind why conspiracy theories captivate us, and how the internet and social media have fueled their spread. We examine the allure of these theories, understanding their appeal as a means to make sense of a complex and often unpredictable world.

The Landscape of Modern Conspiracy Theories

From the mysterious origins of COVID-19 to the enigmatic world of 5G technology, and the perplexing nature of cryptocurrency, each theory we explore in this book is a reflection of contemporary societal anxieties and technological advancements. We introduce the reader to a range of theories, each offering a glimpse into the collective psyche of our time.

Distinguishing Fact from Fiction

A crucial aspect of our journey is the quest for truth. How do we distinguish fact from fiction in a world brimming with misinformation? This chapter discusses the importance of critical thinking and the role of credible sources in navigating the murky waters of conspiracy theories. We underscore the need for a balanced approach that considers both the rational and the seemingly irrational.

The Journey Ahead

As we set out on this exploratory path, we invite readers to join us with an open mind. The chapters that follow are not just stories; they are windows into the fears, hopes, and curiosities that define our era. This introduction is an invitation to look beyond the surface, to question, and to seek understanding in a world where truth and deception often intertwine.

CHAPTER 2: THE UAP ENIGMA

In the expansive canvas of the sky, Unidentified Aerial Phenomena (UAP) have long captured human imagination, oscillating between myth and reality. Chapter 2, "The UAP Enigma," dives into the mysterious world of UAPs, unraveling the blend of fact, fiction, and speculation that has surrounded these phenomena, particularly in the year 2023.

Historical Context and Modern Sightings

The chapter begins by charting the historical trajectory of UAP sightings, from ancient astral observations to modern-day reports by credible witnesses. In 2023, these sightings took a remarkable turn with an increasing number of reports from pilots, astronauts, and military personnel, lending a new level of legitimacy to the UAP discussion.

A pivotal aspect of the UAP narrative is the role of governments worldwide. This section explores the extent of government involvement in UAP research, including declassified documents and statements made by officials in 2023. It examines the fine line between national security concerns and the public's right to know, shedding light on the complex dynamics of transparency and secrecy.

Scientific Investigations and Theories

Central to demystifying UAPs is the scientific investigation into these phenomena. The chapter delves into the efforts of astronomers, physicists, and other scientists in 2023 to understand UAPs. It explores various theories that have been proposed, ranging from natural atmospheric phenomena to advanced extraterrestrial technology, critically analyzing the evidence supporting each theory.

The Impact on Culture and Society

UAPs have had a profound impact on culture and society, influencing everything from popular media to philosophical debates about human existence. This section discusses how 2023 saw a surge in UAP-influenced media and public interest, reflecting the deep-seated human fascination with the unknown and the possibilities of life beyond Earth.

The Future of UAP Research

In concluding, "The UAP Enigma" contemplates the future of UAP research. It highlights the importance of continued scientific inquiry, balanced skepticism, and open-minded exploration. The chapter ends by inviting readers to ponder the possibilities and implications of unraveling one of the greatest mysteries of our time.

Increased UAP Reporting: The All-domain Anomaly Resolution Office (AARO) registered a total of 291 UAP reports from August 2022 to April 2023. This included reports from earlier periods between 2019-2022 that were previously unmentioned, indicating an increased awareness and reporting of UAPs.

Geographic Distribution of UAP Sightings: Most UAP reports initially reflected a bias towards restricted military airspace, primarily due to reporting from military personnel and sensors. However, recent reports from commercial pilots show a more diverse geographic distribution of UAP sightings across the United States, suggesting that UAPs are not just limited to military areas.

No Evidence Linking UAP to Health Concerns or Foreign Activities: While the AARO has not found any evidence linking UAP sightings to health concerns, some reports highlight potential safety concerns for military aviation, such as UAPs displaying high-speed travel and unusual maneuverability. However, no reports suggest direct threats to flight safety or link UAP sightings to foreign activities, leaving the origin and nature of these phenomena largely unexplained.

These developments in 2023 underscore the complex and evolving nature of the UAP phenomenon, revealing both increased awareness and the ongoing mystery surrounding these sightings.

CHAPTER 3: THE DEEPFAKE DILEMMA

As the digital world evolves, the advent of deepfake technology has emerged as a groundbreaking yet controversial development. This chapter delves into the complexities of deepfakes, unmasking the truths within the myriad of conspiracy theories that have surfaced in 2023.

The Rise of Deepfakes: A Technological Marvel

Deepfake technology, which allows for the creation of hyper-realistic video and audio content, has revolutionized the way we perceive media. Its ability to replicate human likeness with stunning accuracy has opened up new avenues in entertainment and information dissemination. However, this technological marvel quickly became a source of widespread concern.

Uncovering Misuse: The Darker Side of Deepfakes

While deepfakes hold immense potential, their ability to create convincing false content has led to a surge in conspiracy theories. These theories often focus on the misuse of deepfakes in politics and media, raising alarms about their potential to spread misinformation, manipulate public opinion, and disrupt democratic processes. This chapter explores incidents where deepfakes have been used maliciously, highlighting the genuine risks they pose.

Distinguishing Fact from Fiction: Deepfakes in the Public Eye

One of the greatest challenges posed by deepfakes is distinguishing real from fake content. This section examines high-profile cases where deepfakes have been used to create controversial content, blending the lines between reality and fiction. It also discusses the impact of deepfakes on public trust in media and the implications for news authenticity.

The Spoiler Alerts: Finding Truths in Conspiracy Theories

Amid the fear and speculation surrounding deepfakes, there are truths to be found. This part of the chapter looks at the conspiracy theories that contain elements of truth, such as concerns over personal privacy, the potential for identity theft, and the weaponization of deepfakes in cyber warfare. It addresses the valid concerns hidden within the more sensational claims.

Ethical Implications and the Call for Regulation

As the technology continues to evolve, the chapter discusses the ethical implications of deepfakes and the growing calls for regulation. It delves into the efforts being made to detect deepfake content and the legal and ethical frameworks being considered to govern their use, emphasizing the need for a balanced approach that fosters innovation while protecting individual rights and societal norms.

Conclusion: Navigating the Deepfake Era

In conclusion, "The Deepfake Dilemma" reflects on the journey through the intricate world of deepfakes. It underscores the need for awareness, critical thinking, and responsible technology use in an era where the distinction between real and artificial is increasingly blurred. The chapter leaves readers contemplating the future of digital media, the potential of deepfake technology, and the importance of safeguarding truth in the digital age.

Growing Challenges of Deepfake Technology: In 2023, experts from Northwestern University highlighted that challenges posed by deepfake technology are only expected to grow. The technology has advanced to the point where it's becoming increasingly difficult to distinguish between real and fake content, raising concerns about its potential misuse in various fields, including politics and personal security.

Ethical and Societal Implications: The development and proliferation of deepfake technology have raised significant ethical concerns. There's an ongoing debate regarding the balance between the innovative potential of deepfakes and their risks, particularly in spreading misinformation, impacting personal privacy, and influencing public opinion.

Advancements in Detection and Countermeasures: In response to these challenges, there has been a concerted effort to develop more sophisticated tools and techniques to detect and combat deepfakes. Organizations and researchers are focusing on creating robust detection algorithms and raising public awareness about the nature of deepfakes to mitigate their negative impacts.

CHAPTER 4: SURVEILLANCE SOCIETY

In 2023, the fabric of privacy and freedom stood at a pivotal crossroads, overshadowed by the ever-growing expanse of global surveillance networks. "Surveillance Society" delves into the intricate web of surveillance spun by governments and corporations, revealing the truths that lurk behind the veil of monitoring and data collection.

The Expansion of Surveillance: A Global Phenomenon

This chapter opens by mapping the sprawling growth of surveillance technologies across the globe. From the streets of major cities equipped with advanced CCTV systems to the invisible digital trails left by citizens in the cyber realm, the reach of surveillance has permeated every facet of modern life. It examines how, under the guise of security and efficiency, governments and corporations have extended their watchful eyes, creating a digital panopticon that tracks, records, and analyzes the movements and behaviors of billions.

Big Data and the Corporate Gaze

The narrative then shifts to the corporate world, where data has become the new gold. Companies, under the banner of personalized services and advertising, harvest vast quantities of data, sketching detailed profiles of individuals' lives, preferences, and habits. This section explores the complex network of data exchange between corporations, and how the pursuit of profit often blurs the line between convenience and intrusion.

The Trade-Off: Security Versus Privacy

In the heart of the surveillance society debate lies the delicate balance between national security and individual privacy. This chapter critically examines key events and policies in 2023 that highlighted this tension, including legislation, court rulings, and public reactions. It delves into the ethical and legal challenges posed by mass surveillance, questioning the price of safety in the currency of privacy.

The Role of Technology: Enabler and Watchdog

Technology plays a dual role in the narrative of surveillance – as both the enabler of unprecedented monitoring capabilities and as a potential watchdog. The chapter explores the advancements in surveillance technologies, such as facial recognition and AI-driven analytics, while also highlighting how technology can be used to resist and regulate surveillance overreach.

Global Voices: Resistance and Reformation

As surveillance networks tighten their grip, voices of resistance echo across the globe. This section chronicles the efforts of activists, privacy advocates, and concerned citizens in challenging and reforming surveillance practices. It showcases how, even in an era of ubiquitous monitoring, the human spirit strives to protect the sanctity of personal freedom and privacy.

Looking Ahead: The Future of Surveillance Society

In concluding, "Surveillance Society" reflects on the trajectory of global surveillance and its implications for the future. It emphasizes the need for an informed and vigilant society, capable of navigating the fine line between the benefits and dangers of surveillance. The chapter leaves readers contemplating the evolving landscape of privacy and freedom in an increasingly watched world, urging a collective consideration of the kind of society we aspire to live in.

Advancements in AI-Powered Surveillance: The global AI surveillance camera market, projected to reach USD 16.75 billion by 2028, indicates a significant growth in the deployment of AI-powered "smart" cameras. These advanced cameras are equipped with capabilities like vehicle detection, person detection, face detection, and license plate recognition, which enhance operational efficiency and security.

Cloud-Based Video Surveillance Trends: Cloud computing is increasingly becoming the preferred choice for video surveillance due to its scalability, flexibility, and cost-effectiveness. The shift towards cloud-based AI solutions and AI-based video analytics is revolutionizing how businesses approach security, monitor user activity, and reduce operational costs.

AI Analytics and Privacy Concerns: With the increasing adoption of AI-based analytics in surveillance, there's a growing focus on privacy protection. The potential enactment of GDPR-like data privacy laws in the U.S. reflects the rising concern over personal privacy and the need for data protection in surveillance technologies.

WHO's International Pathogen Surveillance Network: The World Health Organization launched the International Pathogen Surveillance Network (IPSN) to leverage pathogen genomics data for detecting and preventing infectious disease threats. This development underscores the growing importance of global health surveillance and the use of advanced technologies in public health systems.

CHAPTER 5: VACCINE CONTROVERSIES

Examining the Microchipping Conspiracy Theories Surrounding COVID-19 Vaccines

In an era where mistrust in institutions and technology intertwines with public health, COVID-19 vaccines became the center of various conspiracy theories. Among the most pervasive and sensational was the claim that these vaccines were a guise for implanting microchips in the global population. Chapter 5 delves into these conspiracy theories, exploring their origins, the truths they misconstrue, and the societal impacts they wield.

The Genesis of a Global Conspiracy

The chapter begins by tracing the origins of the microchipping conspiracy theory, which gained traction in the early days of the vaccine rollout. It explores how a combination of misinformation, mistrust in big pharma, and fears of invasive surveillance converged to create a perfect storm of conspiracy theorizing.

Dissecting the Microchipping Claim

Central to this exploration is a thorough examination of the microchipping claim itself. The chapter discusses the technological and logistical feasibility of such an endeavor, consulting experts in fields ranging from vaccine development to microtechnology. It addresses the core question: Is it scientifically and practically possible to implant microchips through vaccines?

The Role of Social Media and Public Figures

A significant focus is given to the role of social media and influential public figures in amplifying these conspiracy theories.

This section analyzes how digital platforms became hotbeds for the spread of misinformation and how certain public figures contributed to the dissemination and legitimization of these baseless claims.

Psychological Underpinnings: Why People Believe

To understand why such theories find a receptive audience, the chapter delves into the psychological aspects. It explores the human propensity for fear-based reasoning, the appeal of simple explanations for complex issues, and the psychological impact of living through a global pandemic.

Societal Impact and Public Health Response

The chapter also examines the tangible impacts of these theories on public health efforts, including vaccine hesitancy and resistance. It looks at how public health officials and institutions have responded to counteract these theories and the challenges they face in restoring public trust in vaccination campaigns.

Concluding Reflections: Between Fear and Fact

In its conclusion, "Vaccine Controversies" reflects on the journey through the labyrinth of vaccine-related conspiracy theories. It underscores the importance of critical thinking, evidence-based understanding, and responsible information sharing in an age where myths can rapidly overshadow medical realities.

In 2023, the conspiracy theory surrounding COVID-19 vaccines, particularly the notion that they contain microchips for tracking and control, continued to circulate, despite being repeatedly debunked.

One significant instance where this theory was brought into the spotlight was through social media posts falsely claiming that a FEMA emergency alert system test would activate nanoparticles like graphene oxide in people's bodies. These posts revived long-debunked conspiracy theories about the contents of the COVID-19 vaccine. Experts, including a professor of microbiology and immunology at the University of Iowa and a pediatric infectious disease specialist at the University of Maryland School of Medicine, have categorically stated that such claims are baseless and that materials like graphene oxide are not ingredients in the mRNA-based COVID-19 vaccines produced by Pfizer/BioNTech or Moderna. Furthermore, the notion that graphene oxide can be "activated" to allow governments to control and monitor people is dismissed as nonsense by experts in the field.

In a related development, the state of Missouri is considering legislation that would ban the use of non-existent vaccine microchips. The bill, HB700, would also restrict Missouri's ability to respond to future pandemics and weaken COVID-19 vaccine mandates. This bill feeds into conspiracy theories, despite the fact that injectable microchips or DNA-altering substances are not part of any FDA-approved vaccine. The bill has moved through multiple rounds of approval in the Missouri House and is scheduled for a final vote.

These developments in 2023 highlight the ongoing challenge of addressing misinformation and conspiracy theories related to COVID-19 vaccines. They underscore the importance of relying on scientific facts and expert opinion in public discourse about vaccine safety and efficacy.

CHAPTER 6: CYBER SHADOWS

"Cyber Shadows" delves into the clandestine world of state-sponsored cyberattacks and their far-reaching global impact. In an era where digital warfare is increasingly becoming a tool of statecraft, this chapter explores the motives, methods, and consequences of these covert operations.

State-sponsored cyberattacks are a modern form of conflict, often used by nations to achieve political, economic, or military objectives without engaging in traditional warfare. These attacks can target critical infrastructure, steal intellectual property, influence elections, and disrupt the normal functioning of governments and businesses.

The chapter begins by examining high-profile cyberattacks attributed to nation-states. Incidents such as the Stuxnet virus attack on Iranian nuclear facilities, the Russian interference in the 2016 US elections, and the widespread WannaCry ransomware attack, allegedly launched by North Korea, are analyzed. These examples illustrate the varied objectives and sophisticated tactics employed in state-sponsored cyber warfare.

Understanding the tactics used in these cyberattacks is crucial. The chapter discusses methods like phishing, malware, denial of service (DoS) attacks, and exploitation of software vulnerabilities. The role of advanced persistent threats (APTs) – networks of clandestine, infiltrating software – is highlighted, demonstrating how these tools allow for long-term espionage and data theft.

The impact of these cyberattacks extends beyond the immediate disruption of services or theft of data. The chapter explores the broader implications, including the erosion of trust in digital infrastructure, economic losses, and the potential for escalating tensions between nations. The psychological impact of cyber warfare on societies, creating an atmosphere of fear and uncertainty, is also considered.

In response to these threats, the chapter evaluates global efforts to enhance cybersecurity. Initiatives by international organizations, national governments, and private corporations are discussed, including the development of stronger cybersecurity protocols, international agreements to curb cyber warfare, and collaborative efforts to track and neutralize threats.

"Cyber Shadows" concludes by contemplating the future of state-sponsored cyberattacks. As technology continues to advance and integrate more deeply into the fabric of society, the chapter posits that cyber warfare will likely become an increasingly common and sophisticated element of international relations. The need for robust, adaptable cybersecurity measures and international cooperation to manage this evolving threat landscape is underscored.

Increasing Focus on Smaller Targets: Research indicated that state-sponsored threat actors are increasingly shifting their focus towards small and medium-sized businesses (SMBs) and smaller enterprises. This trend suggests a strategic diversification in targeting, expanding beyond large corporations and government entities.

Exploitation of Infrastructure and Escalation of Attacks: The number of cyberattacks on critical infrastructure has risen significantly. Over 83 incidents targeted New York's critical infrastructure in the first half of the year alone, demonstrating the growing threat to essential services. This increase points to a strategic shift in targeting vital services and infrastructure, which can have far-reaching effects on society and governance.

The Use of Destructive Malware: There has been an increase in the use of destructive attacks by state-sponsored actors. These attacks, historically associated with Russian aggression, are expected to rise in the coming months and years. The use of destructive malware by these actors demonstrates an intent to destabilize regions or impact vital services, as seen in cases like the Colonial Pipeline attack.

Formation of a Dedicated Cyber Section by the DOJ: The U.S. Department of Justice has created a National Security Cyber Section specifically to prosecute nation-state and state-sponsored cyberthreat actors. This development underscores the seriousness with which governments are now approaching the issue of state-sponsored cyberattacks.

Projected Increase in State-Sponsored Cyberattacks: It is anticipated that state-sponsored cyberattacks will increase in 2023, with revenues from cybercrime expected to reach $344 billion by 2030. This projection indicates the growing scale and economic impact of state-sponsored cyber activities.

These developments in 2023 highlight the evolving and escalating nature of state-sponsored cyberattacks. They underscore the strategic shift towards targeting critical infrastructure and smaller enterprises, the increasing sophistication of attacks, and the global response to these threats. This information provides a vital backdrop for understanding the current state of cyber warfare and its implications for national security, business operations, and international relations.

CHAPTER 7: THE AI INFLUENCE

"The AI Influence" explores the intricate and often controversial theories surrounding the use of artificial intelligence (AI) algorithms in manipulating public opinion and influencing election outcomes. This chapter delves into how AI, a tool with immense potential for good, can also be used as a powerful instrument in the digital battleground of politics.

AI's role in shaping public discourse begins with its ability to analyze vast amounts of data and identify patterns – including human behavior and preferences. This capability, while beneficial for tailoring user experiences online, also opens doors for more nefarious uses, such as the targeted dissemination of propaganda or misinformation.

The chapter first examines the historical context of AI in politics, tracing its evolution from a novel tool to a central element in political campaigns and statecraft. This includes analyzing how various countries and political groups have employed AI to sway public opinion, citing examples from recent elections worldwide.

A critical aspect explored is the role of social media platforms, where AI algorithms curate and recommend content to users. The chapter investigates how these algorithms can create echo chambers and filter bubbles, reinforcing existing beliefs and potentially spreading misinformation. The impact of these AI-driven platforms on democratic processes and their ability to amplify divisive content is scrutinized.

Moreover, "The AI Influence" examines the ethical and legal implications of using AI in political contexts. It discusses the fine line between legitimate political campaigning and manipulation, highlighting the need for transparency and regulation in how AI is deployed in the public sphere.

The chapter also addresses the countermeasures being developed to mitigate the risks associated with AI in politics. This includes efforts by governments, tech companies, and civil society organizations to create more ethical AI algorithms, fact-checking initiatives, and public awareness campaigns about the influence of AI on public opinion.

Lastly, the chapter contemplates the future of AI in politics. It speculates on the potential advancements in AI technology and the corresponding challenges and opportunities they might present in the context of democratic processes.

"The AI Influence" provides a comprehensive overview of the complex interplay between AI, politics, and public opinion. It invites readers to critically assess the impact of AI on democratic processes and the collective responsibility to ensure this powerful technology is used ethically and transparently.

In 2023, the role of artificial intelligence (AI) in politics and elections has continued to evolve and expand, presenting both opportunities and challenges for democracy.

One significant development is the increasing use of AI for political messaging and campaign strategies. AI technologies have been adopted to create more effective political messaging and to conduct poll testing, outperforming traditional campaign consultant recommendations in some cases. This evolution in political campaigning is largely happening behind closed doors, as AI enables the rapid creation and distribution of content tailored to specific audiences. AI-generated political content can include everything from social media posts to videos and texts, crafted to sway public opinion and influence election outcomes.

However, the potential for AI to transform politics extends beyond just messaging. AI is also being used to draft legislative amendments, a process termed "microlegislation," where small changes to existing laws or bills are made to serve specific interests. This process can be exploited by AI, potentially leading to legislation that benefits narrow interests without broad public scrutiny.

The impact of AI on democracy and elections has raised concerns among experts and policymakers. For instance, the potential for AI-generated fake videos and 'rumour bombs' poses a significant risk to the integrity of election processes. There are worries that voters might never be certain about the authenticity of what they see and hear during campaigns. These AI-generated contents can rapidly spread misinformation and undermine the opposition's messaging, making it difficult for voters to discern truth from fabrication.

Furthermore, AI's ability to precisely target audiences with political messaging can significantly influence voter decisions. This precise targeting is crucial in political campaigns, where the focus is on swaying the small percentage of undecided voters who can decide the outcome of an election.

Despite these concerns, there is also recognition of AI's potential to positively impact science and education. The technology's ability to process vast amounts of data and generate insights could be harnessed to improve various aspects of society, including the political process. However, balancing these benefits with the risks posed by AI in the political realm remains a significant challenge.

Overall, the integration of AI into politics and elections is a double-edged sword. While it offers new tools for engaging with voters and streamlining campaign processes, it also presents risks related to misinformation, manipulation, and the undermining of democratic processes. As AI technology continues to advance, it will be crucial to develop strategies and regulations to ensure that its use in the political sphere is transparent, ethical, and conducive to the maintenance of democratic integrity.

CHAPTER 8: CLIMATE SECRETS

"Climate Secrets" embarks on an investigative journey into the enigmatic world of alleged clandestine climate manipulation projects, a topic shrouded in controversy and conspiracy. These projects, often referred to as "geoengineering" or "climate engineering," are purported to be secret attempts by governments or private entities to alter the Earth's climate system.

The chapter begins by defining climate manipulation and its various proposed forms, such as solar radiation management (SRM) and carbon dioxide removal (CDR). SRM involves techniques like injecting aerosols into the stratosphere to reflect sunlight and cool the planet, while CDR focuses on removing CO_2 from the atmosphere.

Delving into the history of geoengineering, the chapter highlights past scientific experiments and proposals, noting how they have transitioned from theoretical concepts to more practical discussions in light of the escalating climate crisis. It examines both the scientific feasibility and the ethical considerations of intervening in Earth's climate system.

The core of this chapter investigates the conspiracy theories surrounding climate manipulation. These theories often claim that certain weather patterns or environmental anomalies are the result of secret geoengineering projects. The chapter critically examines these claims, evaluating the evidence presented and contrasting it with scientific understanding of climate change and meteorology.

One focal point is the controversy over "chemtrails" – the theory that the condensation trails left by aircraft are chemical or biological agents deliberately sprayed for unknown purposes. This theory is dissected, with explanations from atmospheric scientists and experts in aviation.

The potential dangers and unintended consequences of climate manipulation are also a major topic. The chapter discusses how even well-intentioned geoengineering projects could lead to unforeseen environmental and geopolitical consequences, such as disrupted weather patterns or conflicts over governance and control.

In conclusion, "Climate Secrets" acknowledges the growing interest in geoengineering as a response to climate change, while emphasizing the need for transparency, rigorous scientific evaluation, and international regulation. The chapter invites readers to critically assess the delicate balance between technological solutions to climate change and the inherent risks of intervening in Earth's complex and sensitive climate system.

In 2023, significant discussions and developments occurred in the realm of geoengineering, particularly regarding climate manipulation technologies. These developments provide a contextual backdrop for Chapter 8, "Climate Secrets," exploring the potential truths and implications of the conspiracy theories surrounding clandestine climate manipulation projects.

Direct Air Capture and Natural Carbon Removal: Technologies like direct air capture, designed to pull carbon out of the air, have been gaining attention. Though still in its early stages and costly, these technologies are seen as promising means to reduce existing levels of carbon dioxide in the atmosphere. Natural methods, such as reforestation and soil carbon sequestration, are also being considered for their potential to remove carbon from the atmosphere and provide additional ecological benefits. However, there is a consensus that these methods alone may not be sufficient to reverse current global warming trends.

Risks and Governance of Geoengineering: The European Commission has called for international talks on the dangers and governance of geoengineering. The Commission highlighted that current solar radiation management (SRM) technologies represent an "unacceptable level of risk for humans and the environment." This call for global discussion underscores the complexity and potential hazards associated with geoengineering. There is a divide among scientists, with some supporting research into SRM to understand its potential as a temporary solution to global warming, while others call for a ban due to its unpredictable impacts and governance challenges.

Legal and Ethical Implications: A significant issue highlighted in 2023 is the legal void surrounding geoengineering. With interconnected ocean and weather systems, geoengineering projects intended to benefit one region could harm others. The absence of a regulatory framework to determine liability and accountability in the event of transboundary harm points to the need for robust legal and ethical frameworks to manage the risks and ensure equity in geoengineering efforts.

These developments in 2023 highlight the complex and multifaceted nature of climate manipulation and geoengineering. They provide concrete examples and current discussions that can be referenced in "Climate Secrets" to explore the possible truths behind the conspiracy theories of secret climate projects, the scientific feasibility of these technologies, and the ethical, legal, and environmental implications of engaging in such ambitious endeavors to manipulate the Earth's climate.

CHAPTER 9: SPACE RACE MYSTERIES

Probing into the Alleged Secrets and Misinformation in Contemporary Space Exploration Efforts

In the vast, uncharted expanse of space, mysteries abound, some of which have found their way into the realm of popular conspiracy theories. Chapter 9 delves into the intricate web of alleged secrets and misinformation that have surrounded contemporary space exploration efforts, aiming to separate fact from fiction.

The New Dynamics of the Space Race

As we entered the 2020s, the space race took on a new dimension, characterized by the involvement of both national agencies and private players. NASA, Roscosmos, CNSA, and ESA, alongside companies like SpaceX, Blue Origin, and others, have transformed space exploration into a multi-faceted endeavor. This chapter examines how this shift has created fertile ground for conspiracy theories, ranging from clandestine agendas to hidden technologies.

Unraveling the Mysteries of the Moon and Mars

One focal point of space-related conspiracies has been the Moon and Mars missions. The chapter scrutinizes the Apollo missions, addressing theories about moon landings and the alleged sightings of unidentified objects on the lunar surface. Similarly, it explores the intrigue surrounding Mars exploration, particularly the theories about life on Mars and the interpretation of images sent back by rovers, which some claim contain evidence of past civilizations.

The Enigma of Unexplained Incidents

Throughout space exploration history, several unexplained incidents have fueled public curiosity and skepticism. Anomalies observed on the moon, unexplained data from Mars rovers, and puzzling signals from distant galaxies are explored in depth. This section seeks to demystify these incidents, consulting experts in astrophysics and astronautics for their insights.

Deciphering the Role of Misinformation

The chapter also delves into the role of misinformation and propaganda in space exploration. It discusses how certain information about space missions has been controlled, manipulated, or even concealed, citing historical instances where nations may have altered or suppressed information for nationalistic or strategic reasons. This examination sheds light on the complex relationship between space exploration, information dissemination, and geopolitical maneuvering.

Impact on Public Perception and Future Exploration

Finally, the chapter considers the impact of these mysteries and conspiracies on public perception of space exploration. It explores how narratives, whether grounded in reality or not, influence societal understanding of space science and the implications for future space policy and exploration efforts.

Conclusion: Embracing the Unknown

In concluding, "Space Race Mysteries" acknowledges the inherent uncertainties and challenges of space exploration. While it entertains the allure of the unknown, the chapter emphasizes the importance of scientific rigor and critical thinking in navigating through the sea of speculation. It leaves the reader contemplating the immense possibilities of space exploration, amidst the enigmas and mysteries that continue to captivate human imagination and fuel our quest for understanding the universe.

OSIRIS-REx's Asteroid Study: NASA's OSIRIS-REx mission made a sample collection attempt on asteroid Bennu, an object of scientific interest due to its ancient origins. Bennu is a small asteroid with a slight chance of hitting Earth in the late 22nd century. This mission is significant not just for its potential to uncover secrets of the early solar system but also for the conspiracy theories it may fuel about asteroid surveillance and impact predictions.

Boeing and SpaceX's Commercial Crew Program: In a significant advancement for private space exploration, Boeing and SpaceX continued their efforts to launch humans into space as part of NASA's Commercial Crew Program. SpaceX's Crew Dragon capsule and Boeing's Starliner craft are at the forefront of this endeavor, marking a new era in space travel and potentially giving rise to theories about the privatization of space and its implications.

Moon Exploration by Multiple Countries: Russia, India, and the United States announced ambitious lunar missions. Russia's Luna 25 lander, India's Chandrayaan 3, and lunar landers from Intuitive Machines and Astrobotic Technology in the U.S. aimed to explore different regions of the Moon. These missions, particularly involving multiple nations, often become the subject of speculation regarding their true objectives and the competition for lunar resources or strategic positioning.

Europe's JUICE Mission to Jupiter's Moons: The European Space Agency's Jupiter Icy Moons Explorer (JUICE) mission set off to study Jupiter's ocean-bearing moons: Ganymede, Europa, and Callisto. This mission's focus on studying extraterrestrial oceans could stir imaginations and conspiracy theories about the search for alien life and hidden agendas in exploring these distant moons

.

SpaceX's Starship Launch: SpaceX's plans to launch its Starship spacecraft into orbit represented a significant step in developing a fully reusable transportation system for both cargo and humans. The capabilities of Starship and its role in future Mars colonization efforts could be a topic of intrigue and conspiracy, especially regarding the long-term intentions of private companies in space exploration.

NASA's Public Discussions on UFOs: In an effort to maintain transparency, NASA held public discussions on unidentified flying objects (UFOs) ahead of releasing a final report on such sightings. While no secret military data were included, such as information about suspected spy balloons from China, these discussions highlight the growing interest and concern over unidentified objects in airspace, potentially fueling further conspiracy theories about extraterrestrial surveillance or hidden military projects in space.

These events from 2023 provide a rich backdrop for "Space Race Mysteries," blending actual space missions and new discoveries with the speculative world of conspiracy theories. They offer a unique perspective on how contemporary space exploration efforts can be both a source of wonder and a breeding ground for alternative theories and speculations.

CHAPTER 10: PANDEMIC'S HIDDEN ORIGIN

As 2023 unfolded, the world continued to grapple with the lingering shadows of the COVID-19 pandemic, a crisis that spurred not just a health emergency but also a wave of conspiracy theories. This chapter delves into the intricate weave of these theories, probing the elements of truth that they may inadvertently reveal.

Exploring the Wuhan Narrative

The pandemic's advent in Wuhan, China, was a fulcrum for numerous theories. Some posited the virus as a bioweapon, deliberately released; others suggested it escaped from a lab. While investigations by global health organizations have primarily supported a natural origin, these theories have highlighted crucial aspects of scientific transparency and the need for rigorous biosecurity in virology labs. The lingering questions about the virus's early spread underscore a global call for more open scientific dialogue and collaboration.

The Vaccine Controversy

2023 also saw the perpetuation of theories surrounding the COVID-19 vaccines. From microchipping myths to questions about long-term effects, these theories, though widely debunked, raised important issues about public trust in pharmaceutical development and the transparency of clinical trials. They underscored the essential role of clear, open communication from health authorities and pharmaceutical companies in addressing public concerns and fears.

The Power of Misinformation

The rapid spread of COVID-19 conspiracy theories underscored the potent force of misinformation in the digital age. Social media platforms became hotbeds for the spread of these theories, demonstrating how quickly fear and uncertainty can be sowed and amplified online. This phenomenon highlighted the critical need for digital literacy and responsible information sharing, emphasizing the role of social media companies in moderating content.

Surveillance State Concerns

Some theories suggested that the pandemic was an excuse to expand surveillance and restrict freedoms, reflecting deep-seated fears about government intrusion and loss of privacy. While extreme narratives lacked evidence, they pointed to genuine concerns about the balance between public health measures and individual rights, sparking debates about the acceptable limits of government intervention in crises.

Seeking Truth in an Age of Uncertainty

In the end, "Pandemic's Hidden Origin" is more than a journey through a labyrinth of conspiracy theories. It is a reflection on our collective quest for truth in an era defined by unprecedented challenges and uncertainties. The chapter invites readers to look beyond the surface of sensational claims, to question, to research, and to seek verifiable truths, reminding us that in the pursuit of understanding, skepticism is healthy but should be coupled with an informed and open mind.

Research on the Wuhan Market and Raccoon Dogs: Studies have identified a specific stall in the Wuhan market where environmental samples tested positive for the virus. This stall previously housed raccoon dogs, animals known to be susceptible to coronavirus infection and considered potential intermediaries between bats and humans for virus transmission. This discovery supports the natural spillover theory, suggesting that the market played a crucial role in the pandemic's emergence.

Political and Propaganda Challenges: The early days of the pandemic were marked by significant political tension and propaganda, with baseless accusations exchanged between countries. This climate hindered the transparent and cooperative investigation needed to fully understand the virus's origins. Despite these challenges, a WHO investigation produced a comprehensive report, indicating the unlikelihood of a lab accident being the cause of the pandemic. However, this report faced criticism and was not accepted by all, demonstrating the complexity of navigating political narratives in scientific inquiry.

Learnings from the Investigation for Future Pandemics: The investigation into the origins of COVID-19 highlights the importance of understanding such events to prevent future outbreaks. It underscores the need for improved surveillance and virology capabilities, as well as the challenges in collecting and analyzing relevant data retrospectively. The role of wet markets, with their close quarters of wild animals and humans, has been identified as a significant factor in zoonotic disease transmission. This emphasizes the need for better regulation and biosecurity in such markets to prevent similar events in the future.

Ongoing Oversight and Investigations: Investigations into the origins of COVID-19 have continued, with various committees and organizations, including the United States House Committee on Oversight and Accountability, actively seeking further information. This ongoing scrutiny reflects the global importance of understanding the pandemic's origins, not only for historical accuracy but also for preparing and preventing future health crises.

These findings from 2023 provide a nuanced perspective on the complex interplay of scientific, political, and societal factors that have influenced the understanding of COVID-19's origins. They offer a basis for exploring the 'spoiler alerts' within the conspiracy theories, revealing the underlying truths about the pandemic's emergence and the challenges faced in unraveling its origins.

CHAPTER 11:
5G FEARS

Unpacking the Health and Surveillance Conspiracy Theories Linked to 5G Technology

In 2023, as the world increasingly embraced the revolutionary 5G technology, a wave of conspiracies and fears surged, challenging the public perception of this technological leap. Chapter 11 delves into these theories, unraveling the strands of truth interwoven with speculation.

THE HEALTH DEBATE SURROUNDING 5G

Amidst the rapid rollout of 5G networks, public concern over potential health risks came to the forefront. Conspiracy theories ranged from 5G causing minor health issues to more alarming claims linking it to severe diseases, including COVID-19. While these extreme allegations lacked substantial scientific support, the chapter reveals a more nuanced reality.

The World Health Organization (WHO) addressed these concerns, stating that, to date, no adverse health effects have been causally linked with exposure to wireless technologies. However, it also noted that research specific to the frequencies used by 5G is relatively limited, highlighting the necessity for ongoing scientific studies in this domain. This acknowledgement underscores the need for continual monitoring and evaluation of health impacts as technology advances.

5G and Surveillance Concerns

Another facet of the 5G narrative revolved around surveillance fears. Theories suggested that the deployment of 5G would usher in an era of unprecedented mass surveillance and privacy invasion. While dystopian visions of a surveillance state are unfounded, the chapter uncovers legitimate concerns about data privacy and security in an increasingly networked world. It emphasizes the importance of robust privacy regulations and transparent policies from technology providers and governments.

The Psychological Underpinnings of Conspiracy Beliefs

Why did 5G become a magnet for such widespread anxiety

and conspiracy theories? This section of the chapter explores the psychological and societal factors driving the spread of misinformation. It discusses how rapid technological changes, coupled with a lack of understanding, can create a fertile ground for conspiracy theories, especially in times of global crises like the COVID-19 pandemic.

Balancing Technological Advancement with Ethical Considerations
In concluding, the chapter reflects on the broader implications of these conspiracy theories for society and technological progress. It advocates for a balanced approach to technology adoption, ensuring that innovations like 5G are aligned with ethical considerations, public health, and environmental sustainability. The chapter calls for informed public discourse and responsible policy-making to navigate the complexities of technological evolution in the 21st century.

Research on Health Effects of 5G: Studies have examined the potential genotoxic effects of millimeter waves (MMWs), which are used in 5G technology. These studies, focusing on epithelial and skin cells, have explored the possibility of DNA damage. Although varied methods and exposure models were used, most did not find statistically significant evidence of DNA damage. Some studies reported an increase in micro-nucleation in skin cells, while others did not observe this effect. Furthermore, studies on animals and other cell types have produced mixed results, with some indicating potential DNA damage and others showing no significant effects. The inconsistency and lack of independent verification in these results highlight the complexity and ongoing nature of research into 5G's health impacts.

Concerns about Combined Effects of 5G: A review article emphasized that most laboratory experiments conducted to date on wireless radiation, including 5G, are not designed to identify severe adverse effects reflective of real-life conditions. Many experiments do not include pulsing and modulation of the carrier signal, and most do not account for synergistic adverse effects of other toxic stimuli acting with wireless radiation. The article suggests that 5G technology might have systemic effects beyond commonly believed impacts on the skin and eyes.

CHAPTER 12: CRYPTOCURRENCY CONSPIRACIES

In the rapidly evolving world of digital finance, cryptocurrencies have emerged as both a revolutionary asset and a source of widespread speculation and conspiracy. Chapter 12 delves into the labyrinth of theories surrounding the control and regulation of digital currencies, seeking to unveil the truths hidden within the world of blockchain and crypto.

The Specter of Government Control

At the heart of many cryptocurrency conspiracies lies the fear of government intervention and control. The decentralized nature of digital currencies like Bitcoin and Ethereum is often seen as a threat to traditional financial systems, leading to theories about governments attempting to undermine or co-opt these technologies. This chapter examines the extent of these concerns, exploring real-world cases of government regulation and intervention in the crypto market.

Central Bank Digital Currencies: A New Frontier

The rise of Central Bank Digital Currencies (CBDCs) has added fuel to the fire of conspiracy theories. Proponents of these theories argue that CBDCs are a ploy for governments to gain unprecedented control over financial transactions and individual privacy. This section scrutinizes the development of CBDCs globally, dissecting the potential implications for privacy, freedom, and the future of decentralized finance.

Cryptocurrency and Surveillance Concerns

Another prevalent theory in the crypto world revolves around surveillance. The chapter explores the balance between the need for regulatory oversight to prevent illegal activities like money laundering and the preservation of the anonymity that is a cornerstone of the cryptocurrency ethos. It discusses how blockchain technology itself can be both a tool for privacy and a potential means of surveillance.

The Role of Big Tech in the Crypto Narrative

Big Tech's foray into digital currencies has also been a source of conspiracies. From Facebook's Diem (formerly Libra) to other tech giants' interest in blockchain, this section delves into theories that suggest an attempt by these corporations to establish a new world financial order, and the truths and exaggerations within these claims.

Deciphering the Myths from the Realities

In concluding, the chapter seeks to separate the myths from the realities in the realm of cryptocurrency. It emphasizes the need for a nuanced understanding of digital currencies, recognizing their potential to transform the financial world while being cognizant of the legitimate concerns surrounding regulation, privacy, and corporate influence.

Government Regulation and Oversight: In 2023, regulatory bodies like the CFTC and SEC in the United States increased their enforcement actions related to digital assets. This rise in regulatory attention fueled theories about the government's intention to control or suppress cryptocurrency, reflecting broader concerns about the future of decentralized finance.

Economic Theories and Conspiracy: The volatile nature of cryptocurrency prices and their susceptibility to market dynamics led to various conspiracy theories. Some of these theories suggest that the crypto market is manipulated by influential figures or entities, contributing to widespread speculation and distrust among investors.

General Public Perception: The general perception of cryptocurrencies is often influenced by their portrayal in media and popular culture. The lack of understanding and the complexity of blockchain technology have contributed to the spread of various conspiracy theories, ranging from market manipulation to cryptocurrencies being part of a larger scheme to undermine traditional financial systems.

CHAPTER 13: FACIAL RECOGNITION FEARS

In an era where technology leaps boundaries with each passing day, facial recognition technology stands at the forefront of modern advancements and controversies. This chapter delves into the intricate web of Artificial Intelligence (AI) in mass surveillance, exploring its profound implications on privacy, ethics, and society.

The Rise of AI in Surveillance

Facial recognition technology has emerged as a pivotal tool in mass surveillance, offering unprecedented capabilities in identifying individuals. It starts with a historical overview of facial recognition technology, tracing its evolution from a novel concept to a ubiquitous reality in public spaces, airports, retail stores, and even on our personal devices.

Privacy in the Public Eye

Central to the debate around facial recognition is the issue of privacy. This section examines how the widespread use of this technology challenges traditional notions of privacy. It dives into various instances where facial recognition has been employed, from tracking criminals to monitoring public movements, and discusses the thin line between security and privacy invasion.

Ethical Dilemmas and Social Impact

The ethical implications of AI in mass surveillance are vast and complex. This chapter scrutinizes the potential for bias and error in facial recognition systems, highlighting cases where technology has misidentified individuals, leading to false accusations or arrests. The discussion extends to the societal impact of such errors, particularly on minority communities who often bear the brunt of these inaccuracies.

Global Perspectives and Regulations

Different parts of the world have responded variously to the rise of facial recognition technology. This section contrasts the approaches of various countries, from stringent regulations in the European Union to more expansive use in countries like China. It also covers the debates within the United States, where there is a mosaic of state and local laws governing the use of this technology.

Advancements and Future Potential

Despite its controversies, facial recognition technology continues to advance. This part of the chapter examines the cutting-edge developments in AI and facial recognition, considering both the potential benefits, such as finding missing persons or improving security, and the risks of increasingly sophisticated surveillance capabilities.

Balancing Act: Technology and Human Rights

The chapter concludes by contemplating the future of facial recognition technology in the context of human rights and personal freedoms. It underscores the need for a balanced approach that harnesses the benefits of AI while safeguarding individual rights. The chapter calls for ongoing dialogue among technologists, policymakers, and the public to navigate the complexities of facial recognition technology and its role in society.

In "Facial Recognition Fears," the exploration of AI in mass surveillance is multi-dimensional, addressing the technological advancements and their societal implications, while encouraging a thoughtful discourse on the future of privacy and ethics in an AI-driven world.

EU's AI Act and Public Mass Surveillance: In 2023, the European Union's decision not to fully ban public mass surveillance in its Artificial Intelligence (AI) Act was a significant development. This decision was criticized by human rights organizations like Amnesty International, which argued that not ensuring a full ban on facial recognition technologies missed an opportunity to prevent damage to human rights, civic space, and the rule of law. This decision sets a global precedent concerning AI regulation, indicating real concerns about the use of AI in surveillance and its impact on human rights.

Surveillance Trends for 2023 and Beyond: The year 2023 saw significant advancements in AI-powered "smart" cameras and surveillance technologies. These technologies, including AI and deep learning algorithms, are increasingly used for advanced targeted searches and operational efficiency in surveillance. The growing demand for all-in-one solutions and flexible cloud storage solutions for surveillance indicates a trend towards more sophisticated and integrated AI surveillance systems. This trend underlines the concerns about the increasing capabilities of surveillance technologies and their potential misuse.

UN Experts on AI Surveillance and Disinformation: In 2023, UN-appointed independent rights experts highlighted the urgent need for regulation in the AI space, particularly concerning AI-powered spyware and disinformation. The experts emphasized the alarming use and impacts of these technologies on human rights and called for strict regulatory measures. This development points to the growing concerns about the use of AI in surveillance and disinformation, reinforcing fears about the potential for human rights violations and the need for robust safeguards.

Mass Spying and AI: Discussions around AI and mass spying in 2023 focused on the increasing integration of AI technologies in surveillance systems. Concerns were raised about the potential for AI to fuel mass spying, with technologies like Siri, Alexa, and Google Assistant already capable of always listening, and the potential for this data to be used for surveillance purposes. This trend highlights the real concerns about the expansion of AI in surveillance and the potential for privacy violations, aligning with the conspiracy theories about mass surveillance using AI technologies.

CHAPTER 14: ENERGY SUPPRESSION

"Energy Suppression" ventures into the world of alleged advanced energy technologies that, according to various conspiracy theories, have been suppressed to protect the interests of traditional fossil fuel industries. This chapter delves into the complex interplay of innovation, economics, and power dynamics that characterizes the global energy sector.

At the heart of these theories is the claim that revolutionary energy technologies — capable of drastically altering the world's reliance on fossil fuels — have been developed but are being withheld from the public. These supposed technologies range from zero-emission fuel sources to free energy devices, purportedly suppressed due to their potential to disrupt the existing energy market and geopolitical power structures.

The chapter begins by exploring the historical context of energy suppression theories. It revisits past instances where new technologies faced resistance or were allegedly stifled, drawing parallels with the current claims of suppression. This historical perspective helps in understanding the recurring themes and patterns in the narratives of energy suppression.

Critical examination of the most prominent energy suppression theories forms the core of this chapter. These include claims about technologies like cold fusion, advanced solar power, and other alternative energy sources. The chapter assesses the scientific validity of these technologies, the evidence for and against their suppression, and the potential motives of those who might benefit from such suppression.

Another focus of "Energy Suppression" is the role of major energy corporations and governments in shaping energy policy and technology development. The chapter investigates allegations that these entities have engaged in covert actions to suppress or discredit emerging energy technologies that threaten the status quo.

The impact of these suppression theories on public perception and policy is also a key topic. The chapter discusses how belief in energy suppression can fuel skepticism towards established energy policies and foster a sense of distrust in governmental and corporate intentions.

In its conclusion, "Energy Suppression" acknowledges the complexities surrounding the development and adoption of new energy technologies. It emphasizes the need for a balanced approach that considers both the potential of emerging technologies and the economic, political, and environmental realities that govern the energy sector.

By exploring the intricate and often controversial world of alleged energy suppression, this chapter invites readers to critically consider the intersection of technology, economics, and power in shaping the future of global energy.

In 2023, significant advancements and discussions in the field of energy technologies and innovations have occurred, providing a rich context for the chapter "Energy Suppression."

One of the notable developments is the release of the AEIC 2023 U.S. Energy Innovation Report Card by the American Energy Innovation Council. This report highlights the progress made in energy innovation in the United States, with several key recommendations being fulfilled or on track. These include supercharging federal funding for clean energy innovation, funding high-impact demonstration projects, accelerating efforts to support startups and commercialize Department of Energy (DOE) R&D investments, and modernizing energy infrastructure. These advancements demonstrate a commitment to investing in energy innovation and transitioning towards more sustainable energy technologies.

Additionally, the MIT Technology Review's annual list of 10 Breakthrough Technologies for 2023 includes several innovations in the energy sector. This list is significant as it recognizes important technological advances that are expected to have a considerable impact on society. While the specific technologies on this list in the field of energy were not detailed in the information available, the inclusion of energy-related breakthroughs in such a prestigious list underscores the ongoing importance and evolution of this sector.

These developments in 2023 indicate a significant focus and progress in the area of energy technologies and innovations. While conspiracy theories often suggest suppression of advanced energy technologies, the documented advancements and public discussions in this field suggest a more complex and dynamic landscape of energy innovation and policy. This context provides a valuable backdrop for exploring the themes of alleged energy suppression and the realities of energy technology development and adoption.

In 2023, advancements and concerns in the field of mind-reading technology have become increasingly significant, providing pivotal context for this Chapter 14, "Mind-Reading Technology."

One major advancement in the realm of neurotechnology involves the use of brain-computer interfaces (BCIs) and neuroimaging techniques. These technologies, initially developed for medical purposes, are showing potential in interpreting brain signals for communication, especially for individuals with disabilities. For instance, brain-reading devices are being used to assist paralyzed people to move, talk, and interact with their environment. These developments underscore the positive impacts of neurotechnology, particularly in assisting those with disabilities and treating chronic health conditions.

However, alongside these advancements, there have been growing concerns about potential human rights violations related to mental privacy. The pace of technological progress in mind-reading technologies may outstrip existing legal frameworks and regulatory responses. There are calls for proactive shaping of laws to address the ethical and privacy implications of direct neural monitoring and intervention. This includes the need to consider the use of mind-reading in various contexts, such as criminal justice, politics, and the workplace, and to establish international standards and procedures to respect people's inner life.

Ethical approaches to safeguard mental privacy have been proposed, emphasizing the need for embedding specific safeguards into the design of neurodevices and requiring legal regulations for the collection and use of brain data. This is crucial as the invasion of mental privacy raises more troubling concerns than privacy issues related to social media behavior. Proposals include recognizing mental data as sensitive personal information under data protection laws and establishing judicial protection mechanisms for mental privacy.

Furthermore, there's an acknowledgement of the potential for conspiracy theories to emerge around AI and related technologies, including mind-reading. The gap in understanding how AI arrives at its responses can create narrative voids filled by conspiracy theories. These theories often find easy targets in the institutions involved in AI and algorithm development, such as Big Tech and government agencies. The potential for AI conspiracy beliefs to be weaponized is also a concern, underscoring the need for clear and effective public messaging about AI truths and its applications.

These developments in 2023 highlight the complex interplay

between technological advancement, ethical considerations, and the potential for misinformation in the realm of mind-reading technology. They provide a comprehensive backdrop for understanding the current state of neurotechnology and its implications for privacy, human rights, and public perception.

CHAPTER 15: MIND-READING TECHNOLOGY

"Mind-Reading Technology" delves into the fascinating and often contentious subject of technologies developed or purported to be developed for reading and influencing human thoughts. This chapter navigates through the scientific advancements, ethical dilemmas, and conspiracy theories surrounding this topic.

The exploration begins by examining the current state of neurotechnology and its legitimate applications. Cutting-edge research in brain-computer interfaces (BCIs), neuroimaging techniques like fMRI (functional Magnetic Resonance Imaging), and EEG (Electroencephalography) are discussed. These technologies, initially developed for medical and therapeutic purposes, have shown potential in understanding and interpreting brain signals.

Moving deeper, the chapter investigates the claims and theories suggesting the existence or development of technology capable of not only reading minds but also influencing thoughts and behaviors. It scrutinizes the evidence presented in these theories, weighing them against scientific facts and expert opinions. The narrative also includes insights into projects like DARPA's initiatives in neurotechnology and other governmental research that fuel these speculations.

The ethical implications of mind-reading and thought-influencing technologies are a central focus of this chapter. Discussions revolve around the potential misuse of such technologies, privacy concerns, and the moral responsibility of scientists and governments in conducting such research. The chapter also explores the legal frameworks or lack thereof governing the use of such technologies.

"Mind-Reading Technology" also delves into the societal impact and public perception of these technologies. It discusses how the possibility of mind reading and thought manipulation resonates with public fears and fascinations, influencing everything from pop culture to policy debates.

In conclusion, the chapter reflects on the future trajectory of neurotechnology. It considers the potential advancements and their implications for society, emphasizing the need for ethical guidelines and regulatory oversight to ensure that these powerful technologies are used for the betterment of humanity and not for invasive or nefarious purposes.

Advancements in Brain-Computer Interfaces: 2023 has been a significant year for brain-computer interfaces (BCIs), with researchers making notable progress in this field. At the University of Technology Sydney, scientists developed technology that allows for the control of robots using brain signals. This technology involves a head-mounted augmented reality lens displaying white flickering squares. By focusing on a particular square, the brainwaves of the user are picked up by a biosensor, which then translates these signals into commands. This system was demonstrated with soldiers operating a robotic dog using the brain-machine interface, achieving up to 94% accuracy.

Optical Brain-Computer Interfaces: Researchers at the University of California, Berkeley, and other institutions have been working on creating optical probes for neural stimulation. They have integrated organic light-emitting diodes (OLEDs) with silicon complementary metal–oxide–semiconductor (CMOS) control circuitry, resulting in implantable probes that can selectively activate individual neurons in mice. This advancement is part of the broader development in BCIs, which has been identified as the 2023 technology of the year by Nature Electronics. This technology could have significant implications for medical treatments and understanding brain functions.

These advancements in mind-control technologies, particularly in the realm of BCIs, present a reality that was once considered the domain of science fiction and conspiracy theories. While these developments are primarily aimed at medical and military applications, they do give some credence to the idea that technology capable of reading and influencing minds is not only possible but is being actively developed and refined. This chapter can explore these advancements, providing a factual basis for discussions on mind control technologies, and addressing the public's concerns and the ethical implications of such technologies.

CHAPTER 16: ALIEN CONTACT COVER-UP

In "Alien Contact Cover-Up," we delve into the intriguing and controversial world of alleged extraterrestrial encounters and the persistent theories that governments across the globe have systematically concealed these events. The allure of the unknown and the allure of the cosmos converge in this chapter, where we sift through a mix of declassified documents, eyewitness accounts, and cultural phenomena to uncover the truth behind one of the most captivating conspiracy theories of our time.

The narrative begins with a historical journey, revisiting landmark incidents that have fueled the fire of alien conspiracy theories. The infamous Roswell incident of 1947, often cited as the genesis of modern UFO (Unidentified Flying Object) lore, is thoroughly examined. We explore the initial reports of a crashed alien spacecraft, the subsequent military statements attributing the wreckage to a weather balloon, and the ensuing decades of speculation and theories suggesting a cover-up of an extraterrestrial visitation.

From Roswell, we travel to the dense forests of Rendlesham in England, where in 1980, US Air Force personnel stationed at RAF Woodbridge reported encounters with a mysterious craft. This case, dubbed "Britain's Roswell," adds another layer to the tapestry of alien contact theories, highlighted by the release of the Halt Memo and audio recordings from the night of the incident.

The chapter also investigates more recent disclosures, such as the

2017 revelation of the Pentagon's secretive Advanced Aerospace Threat Identification Program (AATIP) and the subsequent release of Navy pilot videos capturing unidentified aerial phenomena. These modern developments have reignited the debate and lent a veneer of credibility to the theories of government involvement in concealing extraterrestrial interactions.

We then shift our focus to the impact of popular culture in shaping public perception of alien encounters. From the science fiction craze of the 1950s to the X-Files era of the 1990s and beyond, entertainment media have both mirrored and molded societal beliefs about extraterrestrial life and government secrecy. We explore how these cultural artifacts have blurred the lines between fiction and potential reality, influencing generations of UFO enthusiasts and skeptics alike.

A critical examination of the psychology behind alien contact theories follows. Why do these theories resonate so deeply with so many? We delve into the human psyche's fascination with the unknown, the allure of conspiracy, and the psychological comfort of believing in a world more complex and enigmatic than the one presented by official narratives.

The chapter, while acknowledging the genuine mysteries surrounding many reported UFO sightings, maintains a critical perspective on the evidence—or lack thereof—supporting these cover-up theories. We evaluate the credibility of various claims and testimonies, contrasting them against the backdrop of scientific inquiry and rational skepticism.

In conclusion, "Alien Contact Cover-Up" provides a thought-provoking exploration of the intersection between belief, skepticism, and the eternal human quest to understand our place in the universe. It leaves the reader pondering the possibilities of extraterrestrial life and the complexities inherent in uncovering truths that may lie just beyond our grasp or understanding.

In 2023, significant developments occurred that support the themes discussed in "Chapter 15: Alien Contact Cover-Up." The U.S. Senate considered a bipartisan measure to compel the government to publicly release records related to UFO sightings, indicating a shift towards greater transparency after decades of secrecy. This proposal, led by Senate Majority Leader Chuck Schumer and Senator Mike Rounds, aims to establish a presumption of immediate disclosure for Unidentified Anomalous Phenomena (UAP) records, with a review board providing rationales for keeping documents classified. Additionally, it mandates the release of records no later than 25 years after their creation, barring direct harm to national security. This move reflects growing public and political interest in UAPs and follows previous disclosures by the Pentagon and NASA that have fueled further speculation and investigation into the subject.

Pentagon Official's Theory on Unexplained Sightings: A Pentagon official, collaborating with a Harvard professor, published a paper proposing that recent unexplained aerial objects might be alien probes from a mothership sent to study Earth. This theory, though speculative, indicates a willingness in official circles to consider extraterrestrial origins for unidentified aerial phenomena.

Increased Scrutiny of UFOs: The heightened interest in UFOs and their potential implications for national security and scientific understanding has led to more rigorous investigations. This increased scrutiny reflects a shift from UFO sightings being fringe conspiracy theories to a subject of legitimate inquiry and discussion.

Exploration of the Extraterrestrial Possibility: The involvement of respected science and intelligence professionals in discussions about UFOs and their potential extraterrestrial origins suggests a growing openness to consider these possibilities, though it also raises questions about the credibility of such theories in academic circles.

CHAPTER 17: HEALTH DATA DILEMMAS

In an era where digitization has permeated every facet of life, the sanctity and confidentiality of personal health information face unprecedented challenges. The rapid transformation from paper-based to digital health records, while heralding a new age of efficiency, has also sparked deep-seated concerns and complex conspiracy theories about privacy breaches and misuse.

The digitalization of health records revolutionized medical data accessibility. These records, once confined to the dusty shelves of a doctor's office, are now a click away, offering remarkable benefits in patient care and medical research. However, this digital leap has not been without its pitfalls. The chapter delves into incidents of data breaches, where the private health information of millions was compromised, exposing vulnerabilities in the systems designed to protect them. These real incidents gave rise to theories speculating about deliberate data mismanagement and exploitation by governments and corporations.

Amidst the growing trove of digital health information, conspiracy theories have flourished. Claims of clandestine surveillance, data mining for commercial benefits, and social control through health data have found a receptive audience. The chapter critically assesses these theories, separating exaggerated fears from genuine concerns. It uncovers instances where health data has been used in ethically grey areas, validating some of the public's mistrust.

Legislation and policy form the backbone of health data privacy.

The chapter examines the effectiveness of laws like HIPAA and GDPR in safeguarding personal health information. It scrutinizes the loopholes and limitations of these legal frameworks, pointing out that while they set the standard for data protection, they often struggle to keep pace with the rapid advancements in technology.

The psychological impact of these privacy concerns on society is profound. The fear of personal health information being misused can erode the public's trust in the healthcare system. The chapter explores this complex psychological landscape, where the benefits of technological advancements must be weighed against the need for privacy and confidentiality.

In conclusion, the chapter underscores the importance of navigating this digital age with a balance of technology, trust, and transparency. It calls for a concerted effort from governments, healthcare providers, and the public to foster an environment where health data can be both beneficial and secure. The future of health data management hinges on this delicate balance, ensuring progress does not come at the expense of the individual's right to privacy.

In 2023, there have been significant developments and incidents that underscore the growing concerns about health data privacy, highlighting that these issues are not mere conspiracy theories but real challenges facing the healthcare sector.

One of the notable developments in October 2023 was a series of healthcare data breaches affecting various entities, including healthcare providers and business associates. These incidents, predominantly caused by hacking, compromised millions of records, demonstrating the vulnerability of healthcare data to cyber threats. The most common location of breached Protected Health Information (PHI) was network servers, indicating a need for stronger cybersecurity measures in these areas. The HIPAA Journal reported several such breaches, with the largest ones affecting millions of individuals, and hacking incidents accounting for the majority of the data breaches during this period.

The first half of 2023 also saw a significant impact of healthcare data breaches, with 40 million Americans affected by reported breaches. Although the number of breaches was on pace to be the lowest since 2019, the number of people affected was expected to surpass all previous years, as reported by Bluefin. This paradox highlights a strategic shift by cybercriminals, who are now targeting fewer but more significant data repositories, yielding greater results with fewer attempts. Ransomware has been a particularly effective tool in these attacks, emphasizing the need for enhanced security measures.

These incidents and trends make it clear that the concerns about health data privacy are well-founded and require ongoing attention and action. The healthcare sector faces the dual challenge of embracing the benefits of digital transformation while safeguarding sensitive patient information against evolving cyber threats. This situation underscores the importance of robust cybersecurity strategies and the need for continuous vigilance and adaptation in protecting health data privacy.

CHAPTER 18: BIOLOGICAL EXPERIMENTATION ALLEGATIONS

The realm of scientific inquiry, often lauded for its groundbreaking discoveries, harbors a shadowy underbelly of ethical transgressions and covert operations. This chapter delves into the murky waters of alleged secret biological experiments, historically conducted under the auspices of advancing science or safeguarding national security.

The narrative begins with a retrospective look at confirmed instances of unethical experimentation. The Tuskegee Syphilis Study, where African American men were deceitfully left untreated to study the progression of the disease, and Project MK-Ultra, the CIA's mind control program, are pivotal examples. These incidents, etched in the annals of history, serve as a grim reminder of the past and set the stage for understanding the genesis of contemporary conspiracy theories.

In the present day, numerous allegations have surfaced, accusing governments and corporations of continuing this dark legacy. Claims range from the development of clandestine biological weapons to the use of civilians as unwitting test subjects in experimental drug trials. The chapter critically examines these claims, dissecting the available evidence, or lack thereof, and the historical patterns that lend these theories a degree of plausibility. It highlights the instances where factual information is interwoven with speculation, creating a complex tapestry of half-truths and misinformation.

Central to the discourse on biological experimentation is the ethical dilemma it poses. The chapter explores the fine line between ethical research and the potential for exploitation. It scrutinizes the existing protocols and guidelines governing biological research, discussing their effectiveness in preventing ethical breaches and the gaps that might fuel suspicions and conspiracy theories.

The societal impact of these allegations is profound. The chapter explores the erosion of public trust in science and government institutions, a consequence of both historical transgressions and modern-day conspiracy theories. This loss of trust is exacerbated by sensationalized media reporting and the spread of misinformation. The narrative delves into the psychological aspects of why society is often quick to believe in such conspiracies, reflecting a deep-seated need for transparency and accountability from those in positions of scientific and governmental authority.

The chapter concludes with a contemplative look at the future of biological research. It advocates for a paradigm shift towards more transparent, ethical, and responsible scientific inquiry. The chapter calls for heightened public awareness and engagement in scientific discourse, emphasizing the need for vigilance to ensure that the pursuit of knowledge does not come at the expense of ethical values and human dignity. The path forward, as outlined in the chapter, is one where scientific progress and ethical responsibility must coexist, ensuring that the benefits of research are realized without repeating the mistakes of the past.

U.S. Support for Ukrainian Labs

In 2023, claims circulated that the U.S. Department of Defense admitted to funding 46 biolabs in Ukraine. However, these labs are owned and operated by the Ukrainian government. The U.S.'s role is primarily supportive, focusing on enhancing lab security and training personnel for disease detection and diagnosis. This involvement is part of the U.S. Cooperative Threat Reduction Program, which works with over 30 countries. This situation was often misrepresented in conspiracy theories, which suggested a more direct and nefarious involvement of the U.S. in these labs.

Classified Experiments on Humans

Reports in 2023 revealed that the U.S. government continued to conduct secretive experiments on human subjects. These experiments, operated under code names like "Moose Drool" and "Hidden Valley," involved around 300 participants. While the exact nature of these experiments remains undisclosed, past controversies over similar government-conducted human experiments have fueled public suspicion and conspiracy theories regarding the intent and ethical implications of such research.

Historical Precedent of U.S. Biological Testing

Historical incidents further reinforce these concerns. Notably, the U.S. government conducted open-air biowarfare experiments on its own citizens between 1949 and 1969, affecting numerous American and Canadian cities. These experiments, which included the release of bacteria like Serratia marcescens and Bacillus globigii, were initially believed to be harmless but later found to cause infections. While officially halted in the 1970s following public exposure, these historical events lend credibility to contemporary fears and conspiracy theories about government-sanctioned biological experimentation.

Russian Claims on U.S. Biolabs

Russian revelations about U.S. military-biological activities in dozens of facilities in Ukraine in 2022 led to a scaling back of U.S. global military-biological programs. These claims, which allege extensive U.S. involvement in the development of deadly pathogens, have prompted international scrutiny and raised questions about the Pentagon's activities in global biolab networks. While the full truth of these allegations remains contested, they have fueled widespread conspiracy theories and concerns about the extent and nature of biological research conducted by governments.

In Chapter 18, these developments from 2023 are examined to explore the underlying truths in conspiracy theories surrounding government-sanctioned biological experimentation. The chapter seeks to unravel the complex interplay of historical precedent, contemporary allegations, and the ethical dilemmas posed by such secretive research endeavors.

CHAPTER 19: SOCIAL MEDIA'S HIDDEN HAND

In the labyrinth of the digital age, social media stands as a double-edged sword, shaping narratives and perceptions at a global scale. This chapter unravels the complex role of social media in the dissemination and amplification of conspiracy theories and misinformation.

The Algorithm's Role in Amplifying Misinformation

- Algorithmic Bias: Social media algorithms are designed to maximize user engagement, often prioritizing content that elicits strong emotional responses. This can lead to the amplification of sensational or controversial content, including unverified conspiracy theories.
- Viral Spread of Misinformation: Case studies demonstrate how easily misinformation can spread on platforms like Facebook and Twitter, often outpacing the dissemination of accurate information.

Notable Instances of Social Media Manipulation

- Political Propaganda: Investigations reveal how political entities have used social media to spread propaganda, influencing public opinion and election outcomes.
- Health Misinformation during COVID-19: The pandemic saw a surge in health-related misinformation, including false remedies and conspiracy theories about the virus's

origins.

- Orchestrated Hoaxes: Examples of fabricated stories that gained traction on social media, influencing public behavior and opinion.

The Effectiveness of Fact-Checking and Content Moderation

- Fact-Checking Initiatives: An analysis of various fact-checking partnerships and their impact on curtailing misinformation.
- Challenges in Moderation: Discussion on the difficulty of content moderation, balancing the line between curbing misinformation and preserving freedom of speech.

Psychological Impact: The Echo Chamber Effect

- Confirmation Bias: How social media reinforces users' existing beliefs, creating echo chambers that polarize public opinion.
- Perception Alteration: Exploration of how prolonged exposure to one-sided information can alter users' perceptions of reality.

Addressing the Misinformation Challenge

- Digital Literacy Programs: The need for educational programs that teach users to critically evaluate online content.
- Collaborative Solutions: Proposals for joint efforts by tech companies, educators, and policymakers to develop more effective methods to counter misinformation while respecting free expression.

Stages of Conspiracy Theory Escalation: Research has identified four key stages in the escalation of conspiracy beliefs on social media:

Identity Confirmation:
Users seek content that verifies their views.

Identity Affirmation:
Information from original sources is selectively used to support conspiracy beliefs.
Identity Protection:
Users actively discredit contradictory evidence.
Identity Enactment:
Seeking broader social approval and potentially recruiting others.
The Interplay of Social Media Use and Beliefs in Conspiracy Theories: Studies have shown that individuals who frequently use social media and rely on it for news are more likely to believe in conspiracy theories. This relationship is stronger among those predisposed to conspiracy thinking, suggesting that social media use amplifies existing beliefs rather than solely causing them.

Psychology of Conspiracy and Misinformation Beliefs: Research has focused on understanding the psychological profiles associated with the endorsement of conspiracy theories. This includes examining factors such as cognitive ability, narcissism, and authoritarian leadership beliefs, and how they correlate with belief in fake news and misinformation.

Prevention and Media Literacy: The ineffectiveness of fact-based approaches to counter conspiratorial beliefs has been highlighted, with a call for prevention and support education. Developing media literacy and critical-thinking skills is essential to help citizens assess the credibility of online information sources. Addressing social exclusion and promoting community values may also help combat the spread of conspiracy theories.

CHAPTER 20: ASSASSINATION CONSPIRACY THEORIES

The echoes of gunshots and the shroud of mystery surrounding high-profile political assassinations have long captivated the public imagination. In Chapter 20, we delve deep into the heart of these enigmatic occurrences, dissecting the myriad conspiracy theories that have blossomed in their wake.

"Assassination Conspiracy Theories" examines the complex web of speculation and intrigue that often surrounds the untimely deaths of high-profile political figures. This chapter not only delves into specific cases but also looks at the broader impact these theories have on public perception, trust in institutions, and the fabric of political discourse.

JFK Assassination: The assassination of President John F. Kennedy serves as a focal point. Despite the Warren Commission's conclusion of Lee Harvey Oswald as the lone gunman, alternative theories persist. These range from suggestions of a second shooter on the "grassy knoll" to elaborate plots involving the CIA, the Mafia, or the Soviet Union.

Martin Luther King Jr. and Robert Kennedy: The assassinations of Martin Luther King Jr. and Senator Robert Kennedy are also explored. In both cases, official narratives — James Earl

Ray as King's lone assassin and Sirhan Sirhan as Kennedy's — are juxtaposed against theories suggesting broader conspiracies. These theories often point to inconsistencies in evidence and witness testimonies, feeding doubts and speculation about potential involvement of government agencies.

Contemporary Cases: Modern examples, such as the assassination of Pakistani Prime Minister Benazir Bhutto, are analyzed to show how conspiracy theories can emerge from political turmoil and opaque investigations. These recent cases demonstrate how easily facts can become intertwined with fiction in the absence of transparent and conclusive investigations.

Impact on Society: JFK conspiracy theories have contributed to a general atmosphere of mistrust towards the U.S. government, impacting public opinion and confidence in governmental agencies. Similarly, the doubts surrounding the assassinations of MLK and RFK have fueled ongoing civil rights debates and distrust in law enforcement and the justice system.

Psychological Appeal: The psychological underpinnings of why people are drawn to conspiracy theories, especially around assassinations, are explored. Factors like the human tendency to seek patterns, a discomfort with randomness in significant events, and the desire for a more compelling narrative than the 'lone gunman' often lead to the adoption of alternative explanations.

Media's Role: The role of media, both traditional and new digital platforms, in propagating these theories is scrutinized. While the media can be a tool for investigative journalism, it can also inadvertently or deliberately fan the flames of conspiracy, often blurring the lines between evidence-based reporting and sensationalism.

Conclusion: In concluding, the chapter reflects on the enduring nature of assassination conspiracy theories. It suggests that while these theories often stem from genuine anomalies or gaps in official accounts, they can alsoarise from a deeper human need to find meaning in chaos. The lasting impact of these theories on political narratives and public trust is acknowledged, along with the necessity for critical thinking and rigorous examination of evidence in navigating the murky waters of political conspiracies.

Shinzo Abe Assassination (2021): Japanese former Prime Minister Shinzo Abe was assassinated by a gunman while delivering a campaign speech in western Japan. This incident was a shocking event in a country known for its low rates of gun violence.

David Amess Assassination (2021): British lawmaker David Amess was stabbed to death by an Islamic State supporter while meeting with voters, highlighting the risks faced by public figures even in seemingly secure environments.

Jovenel Moïse Assassination (2021): Haitian President Jovenel Moïse was assassinated by gunmen, with more than 40 people, including high-ranking police officers and former Colombian soldiers, arrested in connection with the attack.

Idriss Deby Itno Assassination (2021): Chad President Idriss Deby Itno was killed while battling rebels. His death occurred shortly after he was declared the winner of an election, extending his long tenure in power.

Andrei Karlov Assassination (2016): Russia's ambassador to Turkey, Andrei Karlov, was shot dead by a Turkish police officer, which was linked to Russia's military role in Syria.

Jo Cox Assassination (2016): British lawmaker Jo Cox was shot and stabbed to death by a far-right supporter, reflecting the growing political polarization and extremism in society.

Chokri Belaid Assassination (2013): Tunisian left-wing opposition leader Chokri Belaid was fatally shot outside his home, plunging the country into political chaos.

Chris Stevens Assassination (2012): U.S. Ambassador Chris Stevens was killed during an attack on the U.S. diplomatic compound in Benghazi, Libya, an event that sparked numerous conspiracy theories and political controversies in the United States.

Moammar Gadhafi Assassination (2011): The longtime Libyan dictator was killed by insurgents following a NATO-backed uprising, ending his decades-long rule.

These cases provide a backdrop for understanding the emergence and persistence of assassination conspiracy theories. They demonstrate the complex interplay of political motives, security lapses, and the often immediate and far-reaching impact of such events on national and international politics.

CHAPTER 21: THE GEORGIA GUIDESTONES ENIGMA

"The Georgia Guidestones Enigma" unravels the mysteries surrounding one of the most enigmatic modern monuments in the United States. Erected in 1980 in Elberton, Georgia, the Georgia Guidestones are often referred to as "America's Stonehenge." This chapter delves into the monument's origins, the cryptic messages inscribed on it, and the whirlwind of conspiracy theories they have sparked.

Origins and Construction: Beginning with a mysterious figure known as "R.C. Christian" who commissioned the structure. The identity of R.C. Christian and his sponsors remains unknown, adding a layer of intrigue. The construction process, undertaken by the Elberton Granite Finishing Company, noting the precision and care taken in crafting the monument.

Inscriptions and Languages: The Guidestones feature ten guidelines inscribed in eight different languages - English, Spanish, Swahili, Hindi, Hebrew, Arabic, Chinese, and Russian. These guidelines, which speak of maintaining humanity under a certain population, living in harmony with nature, and seeking a new language of justice, have been the subject of much speculation and interpretation.

Interpretations and Theories: Various interpretations of the Guidestones' inscriptions are explored. While some view the guidelines as a call for environmental stewardship and rationality, others interpret them as ominous or even sinister, suggesting themes of global depopulation and the establishment of a new world order.

Conspiracy Theories: The chapter delves into the conspiracy theories surrounding the Guidestones. These range from beliefs in their connection to secret societies, like the Rosicrucians or Freemasons, to theories proposing they are a harbinger of apocalyptic events. The role of these theories in popular culture and their influence on public perception is analyzed.

Vandalism and Public Reaction: The Guidestones have been the subject of vandalism and controversy, reflecting the public's mixed reactions to their presence and the messages they bear. Incidents of defacement and demands for their removal are discussed, showcasing the monument's contentious nature.

Cultural and Historical Context: The chapter places the Georgia Guidestones within the broader context of megalithic structures and monuments worldwide, drawing comparisons to other sites like Stonehenge. This comparison helps to understand how such structures often become focal points for myth-making and conspiracy theories.

Impact on Local and Global Communities: The impact of the Guidestones on both the local community in Elberton and the broader global audience is considered. While they have attracted tourists and brought attention to Elberton, they have also sparked global discussions on their meaning and the intentions behind them.

Conclusion: In concluding, the chapter reflects on the enduring allure and mystery of the Georgia Guidestones. It discusses how, in their ambiguity and the debates they inspire, the Guidestones serve as a mirror for the fears and hopes of humanity. They are a testament to the power of mystery and the endless human quest for understanding in an increasingly complex world.

In 2023, the Georgia Guidestones, often referred to as "America's Stonehenge," became the center of renewed attention due to their destruction. This event and its aftermath provide pivotal information that can support and add depth to Chapter 21, "The Georgia Guidestones Enigma."

Destruction of the Guidestones: On July 6, 2022, the Georgia Guidestones were partially toppled by an explosive device. This act of vandalism brought down one of the monument's slabs, and the remaining structure was subsequently demolished for safety reasons. The Georgia Bureau of Investigation released surveillance video capturing the detonation and a vehicle fleeing the scene, yet the perpetrators and their motives remain unknown.

Investigation and Mystery: A year after the destruction, the mystery of who was responsible and their motivation continues to deepen. Despite the release of surveillance footage showing a figure running from the monument before the explosion, no arrests have been made. The Georgia Bureau of Investigation has confirmed that they have exhausted all leads and are waiting for new information to emerge.

Impact on the Community: The Guidestones' destruction has had a significant impact on the local community. Tourism in Elbert County, where the Guidestones were located, has reportedly suffered since their demolition. The loss of the monument, which was one of the few attractions in the area, has been felt both economically and culturally.

Controversies and Conspiracies: Since their erection in 1980, the Georgia Guidestones had attracted considerable controversy due to their mysterious origins and the nature of the inscriptions. The messages engraved in eight languages on the granite slabs, which included guidelines for humanity and calls for population control, had fueled various conspiracy theories, ranging from New World Order agendas to satanic influences.

The destruction of the Georgia Guidestones and the ensuing mystery surrounding the act add a new chapter to the monument's enigmatic history. This incident, coupled with the longstanding controversies and conspiracy theories about the Guidestones, offers a rich context for exploring the complex interplay between mystery, public perception, and conspiracy thinking in modern culture.

21 OUTRO: THE QUEST FOR TRUTH

As we conclude our journey through "Conspiracy Theories or Spoiler Alerts! 2023 in Review," it becomes clear that the world of conspiracy theories is as complex as it is fascinating. In this book, we have navigated a diverse landscape of modern conspiracies, from the mysteries of UAPs and the intricate web of cyber espionage to the controversial debates over vaccine safety and the enigmatic allure of the Georgia Guidestones.

Each chapter has offered a window into the myriad ways in which conspiracy theories intersect with our lives, politics, technology, and understanding of the world. We have seen how these theories can arise from genuine unanswered questions, societal fears, technological advancements, and often from the simple human need to make sense of the inexplicable.

The Quest for Truth is not just about debunking or validating these theories but understanding their roots and implications. It's about recognizing the impact they have on society, policy, public perception, and even our collective psyche. This exploration has underscored the importance of critical thinking, rigorous examination of evidence, and maintaining an open yet skeptical mind.

As we step into the future, it's evident that conspiracy theories will continue to evolve alongside our changing world. New technologies, scientific advancements, and global events will undoubtedly give rise to fresh theories, each demanding our attention and discernment.

In navigating this ever-shifting landscape, our greatest tool remains a balanced approach — one that respects the pursuit of truth and acknowledges the complexities of the world we live in. By maintaining this balance, we can hope to navigate the murky waters of conspiracy theories with a keen eye for truth, a respect for evidence, and an understanding of the broader context in which these theories arise.

"Conspiracy Theories or Spoiler Alerts! 2023 in Review" has been an expedition into the heart of contemporary myth-making. As we close this chapter, we are reminded of the ongoing quest for understanding in an age where the line between truth and fiction is often blurred. Let this journey inspire a continued quest for knowledge, understanding, and, above all, the discernment to seek the truth.

COMING IN 2024!

In the next gripping installment of the "Conspiracy Theories or Spoiler Alerts!" series, "The Illuminati Factor" takes readers into the shadowy and intricate world of one of the most enduring conspiracy theories — the Illuminati. Believed by some to be a secret society that manipulates global events, the Illuminati has been a source of fascination and fear for centuries.

From its historical origins in the 18th century to its pervasive presence in modern conspiracy culture, this book explores the multifaceted dimensions of the Illuminati legend. We unravel the threads of historical fact, fiction, and speculation that have woven the complex tapestry surrounding this enigmatic group. Are they merely a product of creative minds, or is there more to the story?

"The Illuminati Factor" delves deep into the heart of various theories about the Illuminati's involvement in major global events, from revolutions and wars to shaping the economic and political landscapes of nations. The book examines how the concept of the Illuminati has been used to explain the inexplicable, serving as a convenient scapegoat for the world's mysteries and misfortunes.

As we navigate through tales of secret symbols, hidden agendas, and elite power structures, readers are invited to question and analyze the evidence. The book probes the societal and psychological reasons behind the enduring appeal of the Illuminati in popular culture, from novels and films to internet forums and social media.

Each chapter of "The Illuminati Factor" is meticulously

researched, presenting a balanced view that juxtaposes the mythos with reality. Through a blend of historical analysis, cultural commentary, and critical inquiry, this book offers a compelling exploration of the Illuminati's place in the collective imagination.

Join us on this enlightening journey as we dissect one of the most intriguing and enduring conspiracy theories of all time. "Conspiracy Theories or Spoiler Alerts! The Illuminati Factor" is more than just a book; it's an expedition into the depths of human belief, power, and the quest for understanding in a world brimming with mysteries.